SYMBIOSIS

Fayez S. Sarofim Research Building, Home of The Brown Foundation
Institute of Molecular Medicine for the Prevention of Human Diseases

ORO *editions*

BNIM Architects

JASON
GOOD LUCK AND
GREAT DESIGN
[signature]

JASON,
THE FUTURE FOR
GOOD DESIGN LOOKS
GOOD.
Mark Shapiro

SYMBIOSIS

Fayez S. Sarofim Research Building, Home of The Brown Foundation
Institute of Molecular Medicine for the Prevention of Human Diseases at
The University of Texas Health Science Center at Houston

Steve McDowell + Mark Shapiro
Introduction by **Andrew Payne + Rodolphe el-Khoury**

DEDICATION

Early in the process of designing the Fayez S. Sarofim Research Building, Home of The Brown Foundation Institute of Molecular Medicine for the Prevention of Human Diseases (IMM), we encountered references to the first leader of the Institute–Hans J. Müller-Eberhard, M.D., Ph.D. We were inspired by what we learned about this man and his contributions to the Institute and to the process of scientific discovery. Hans J. Müller-Eberhard was recruited by President Dr. James T. Willerson, M.D., to The University of Texas Health Science Center at Houston to serve as the Institute's founding director, and in that role he established an atmosphere of collaborative research based on intellectual interaction.

The philosophy and approach that Dr. Müller-Eberhard took toward scientific research and collaboration were the design seeds–planted a decade ago–that make this building an important milestone in the pursuit of buildings that are restorative for human beings and the planet. The progressive leadership of the IMM and the UT Health Science Center established a vision for collaborative science in both the laboratory and the architecture. By embracing that spirit of collaboration, the team created a laboratory founded upon the highest principles of scientific discovery, community, human health, fiscal responsibility and environmental stewardship, enabling the prevention of human diseases.

TABLE OF CONTENTS

A FRAMEWORK FOR DIFFERENCE AND INTERACTION
by Andrew Payne + Rodolphe el-Khoury

The university as a public institution has undergone significant transformation since the philosopher Jean François Lyotard first heralded the emergence of a "postmodern condition" in a report written for the Quebec Conseil des Universités in 1979. Driven by a post-Enlightenment conception of the relationship between theoretical and technical realms of intellectual endeavor, new disciplinary agendas (semiotics, topology, cybernetics, systems theory, robotics, nano-engineering) and novel liaisons between already existing disciplines proliferate within this condition, leaving both humanistic and scientific sectors of the university community significantly transformed. What is more, this transformation is attended by an altered conception of the relationship between the university, as a public corporation, and private-sector interests. The result is a kind of vague epistemological terrain in which disciplinary boundaries are protean and the opportunities for unprecedented forms of collaboration between highly specialized knowledge sectors plentiful. If, at the time Lyotard penned his report, "language" was the privileged semantic locus for this disciplinary realignment, today it is "life," albeit a life reconceived in post-vitalist terms as self-organizing system, which seems to have assumed that role. The Italian philosopher Giorgio Agamben expresses the current intellectual ethos when he says, in an essay published some sixteen years after *The Post Modern Condition,* that "the concept of 'life'...must constitute the subject of the coming philosophy."[1] Concomitant with this shift from language to life, one can observe the emergence of a bio-constructive paradigm in which traditional distinctions between living and artificial systems are progressively dissolved and in which life is increasingly conceived as informational complexity. The challenges and opportunities implied by this dissolution are arguably brought into focus by the Human Genome Project, with its promise of willfully redesigning the constituent elements of the life process in conformity with a perspective that collapses any distinction between biogenetic and informatic regimes. As the cultural theorist and philosopher of science, Eugene Thacker,

observes, the adoption of this paradigm brings both philosophy and science into confluence with a diverse array of all technical fields and commercial enterprises, including genomics, patenting, GM foods and pharmaceuticals.

Enter the Fayez S. Sarofim Research Building, Home of The Brown Foundation Institute of Molecular Medicine for the Prevention of Human Diseases at The University of Texas Health Science Center at Houston. A six-story, 229,000-square-foot structure that incorporates wet and dry research laboratories, administrative offices, conference rooms, open spaces specifically designed for collaborative scientific discussion, a 200-seat auditorium and a large atrium for public events and ambient social interaction, the building takes its name from a donor who gifted the Health Science Center with $25 million for biogenetic research. The Institute's first director and presiding genius of the place, Hans J. Müller-Eberhard, was both a doctor and a research scientist whose career was deeply committed to cross-disciplinary collaboration. This commitment remains a conspicuous feature of the Institute in its current incarnation, which oversees research in a variety of areas, including human genetics, proteomics and bioinformatics. These few facts suggest the degree to which this building and the Institute it accommodates are products of that altered intellectual condition invoked above, with its conflation of vital and informatic regimes, its blurring of boundaries between erstwhile intellectual jurisdictions and its novel confluence of public and private interest. So the question inexorably arises: what sort of architecture would be adequate to this changed intellectual condition and the bioconstructive paradigm currently regnant within it?

Before responding to that question, it is worth observing that architecture was very early to the transdisciplinary ethos, and that its commitment to this ethos has implied, from the start, a nimble two-step between theoretical and practical, humanistic and technical agendas. A glance at Book One of Vitruvius' *De architectura* will serve to suggest just how far this polymathic spirit reaches down into the discipline.[2] As for life, a preoccupation with it and its autopoetic properties can be observed at every step along the architectural way. It is apparent, for instance, in Vitruvius' description of the efflorescence of the human building arts out of the primitive givens determining the life of the species; it passes through Claude Perrault's late-seventeenth-century attempt to apply Descartes' newly minted physics simultaneously to the fields of medicine and architecture; finally, it serves as a thematic counterweight to twentieth-century fascination with industrial mechanization, a counterweight felt in projects as diverse as Le Corbusier's Unité d'Habitation and Eero Saarinen's IBM Thomas J. Watson Research Laboratory. What is more, architecture has been, among the cultural disciplines, the first to elaborate both a theoretical perspective on and practical responses to this bioconstructive paradigm, as is apparent in a range of topics that have animated the discipline over the past decade. To improvise a random sampling from a much larger constellation, that range may be thought to include: post-human architecture, cybercity, biomimicry, biopolitics, non-standard construction, autopoesis, self-organization, emergence, landscape urbanism, rhizomatic–as against arborescent–organization, complexity theory, the green building and the intelligent building. True to their profession, BNIM Architects has a long and distinguished history of cross-disciplinary collaboration, and although their work operates at some distance from the rhetoric associated with the constellation of contemporary topics cited above, their approach, developed over thirty-seven years of practice, represents a considered response to this bioconstructive paradigm. It is an approach that argues in intelligently pragmatic ways for a sustainable imbrication of natural and human systems aided by the most advanced construction technologies. Whereas the current neo-avant garde, taking inspiration from the post-vitalist life philosophy of Gilles Deleuze, has attempted either to give figure to this emergent paradigm or, through the insinuation of hypersurfaced artifacts, to dramatically reshape the modalities of collective conduct associated with its ascendance, BNIM eschew grand rhetorical gestures, preferring to negotiate the most resounding effects of this intellectual and cultural sea-change by the most modest and pragmatic of means. Though deeply invested in cross-disciplinary collaboration and biomimetic integration of living and artificial systems, BNIM construe the architectural question provoked by the current state of university research as simply a variant on a very familiar one: how might a building most generously support the needs and aspirations of the community, of users living and working under this new condition, while at the same time optimizing the reciprocities obtaining between the animate and artificial systems supporting this use?

To judge from the built results, BNIM's response to their own question is twofold. On the one hand, what these postmodern knowledge workers most need and desire is a legible spatial diagram in which the provision of disciplinary specificity is recognized not as an impediment to, but rather as a necessary precondition of, meaningful collaboration between distinct jurisdictions, and in which the accommodation of such specificity is sufficiently flexible to adapt to the protean nature of contemporary intellectual endeavor. On the other hand, what they need and desire is a climatic filter for mediating and rarifying their experience of their surroundings. The result of that twofold response is a "vertical campus" whose lower stratum follows BNIM's preference for open, flexible public spaces which combine the spatial intensity and social focus of a deliberately shaped interior with the freedom and atmospheric amenity of the exterior, and whose upper strata are then given over to accommodating the more specialized activities of the distinct research communities inhabiting the building in the most efficacious, flexible and ecologically responsible manner possible.

Designed as the gateway to a new academic campus, the building internalizes the large open space that forms the heart of the projected campus. Here, the unfolding of the urban savannah is less interrupted than framed, giving discernible form and concentrated presence. This frame takes the form of the building's central atrium, which, inserted between the building's administrative and laboratory wings, serves as the link not only between interior and exterior spaces but also between lower and upper, open and secured strata in this "vertical campus." The atrium is, quite simply, the device that brings all the discrete parts of this machine into sympathy, and its presence dominates the distribution of space and program on the building's layered grounds.

The strategy of clear vertical stratification—as against a more complex imbrication of open and secured spaces—is consistent with the approach to institutional architecture that BNIM has developed. That approach eschews any conception of the building as an integral gestalt, preferring to treat the built object as a kind of machinic assemblage, a dispositif in which each part, unburdened of overriding formal conceits, can be more ably faceted in response to the particular condition or problem it is designed to address. In this case, the stratification of program allows both public and private spaces to be more precisely calibrated to their respective modalities of occupation, with the central atrium then serving as a spine along which these strata are distributed and by which they are brought into communication. Meanwhile, the various circulation devices (stairs, ramps and bridges) that circumscribe and traverse the atrium serve to at once render movement between the building's two specialized sectors, research and administrative, more efficient and to provide exhilarating vistas onto the public scene below, thereby lending a measure of social drama to the professional routines of their users. It is along these generously dimensioned and extensively deployed devices that much of the casual mixing among the community's various constituencies will take place. They provide a mediate scale of social interaction between the privacy of the labs and offices and the public character of the ground floor, which includes a café, an auditorium, conference facilities, lobbies and service areas. These are designed to serve not merely those working in the building but the entire campus community. This floor is organized on a free plan that distributes program in a flexible manner perfectly suited to the diverse demands placed on it by the various communities availing themselves of its services.

This conception of the building as an infrastructural framework that accommodates a kit of specialized parts is also apparent in the approach to the building's façades, which are differentiated in response to both distinct climatic conditions and to the formal peculiarities of the gardens and lawns onto which they face. It is equally apparent in the variable floor elevations on the building's south wing, which serve to accommodate air distribution systems designed to minimize the energy cost of climate control. The result is a flexible building that avails its occupants of all that counts as amenity on the surrounding site, fosters both programmed and spontaneous collective interaction at all scales and provides the research communities working within it with lab spaces that are at once flexible and outfitted for the most specialized and technologically demanding forms of contemporary research.

[1] Giorgio Agamben, "Absolute Immanence," *Potentialities*, trans. Daniel Heller-Roazen, p. 238. Stanford, CA: Stanford University Press, 1999.

[2] Marcus Pollo Vitruvius. "On the Training of Architects." *De architectura* (On architecture), Book 1, c. 1, trans. Frank Granger, p. 9-24 . Cambridge, MA: Harvard University Press, 2002.

"*Reason alone will not serve. Intuition alone can be improved by reason, but reason alone without intuition can easily lead the wrong way. They both are necessary. The way I like to put it is that when I have an intuition about something, I send it over to the reason department. Then after I've checked it out in the reason department, I send it back to the intuition department to make sure that it's still all right. That's how my mind works, and that's how I work. That's why I think that there is both an art and a science to what we do. The art of science is as important as so-called technical science. You need both. It's this combination that must be recognized and acknowledged and valued.*"

Jonas Salk

HORIZONTAL
RAIN WW

GARAGE SECTION

GARDEN
GREEN
HEDGE

OPTIMISM

Scientists, teachers and care providers all share an optimistic and deep commitment to working towards a better future. Each believes that his or her work will have a lasting impact on mankind. The learning, teaching and research that will take place within the IMM will contribute to disease prevention and healthier lives for future generations.

Design is an equally optimistic pursuit. The act of building is too complicated, time-consuming and expensive, unless those involved truly believe in the idea that their efforts will be rewarded in the making of a better world.

the team expressed a commitment to the aspirations of the Institute *and to a dynamic symbiosis between the building, the science and the community.*

The Fayez S. Sarofim Research Building is a catalyst for achieving such a change. From the outset, the team expressed a commitment to the aspirations of the Institute and to a dynamic symbiosis between the building, the science and the community. The mission of the IMM shaped the design, and the design will shape the work of the scientists. The science will challenge the building, and the environment will inform and challenge the science. The IMM and the building will create the community and, over time, the community will give life and form to the science and the building.

Both the IMM's commitment to creating a place that would attract the brightest scientists for many years to come and the design team's concept, which would allow the facility to adapt well into the future, anticipate that this facility will be present to see the best possible outcome—the prevention of human disease. And that is the very embodiment of optimism.

"*Our genes and proteins are the game officials of our lives. They already know if you have a cancer in your future. Or dementia, or some other devastating disease. We must identify these genes and proteins in our bodies and discover ways in which they might be altered to prevent those diseases from occurring in the first place...That research is the role of the IMM.*"

James T. Willerson, M.D., President,
The University of Texas Health Science Center
at Houston

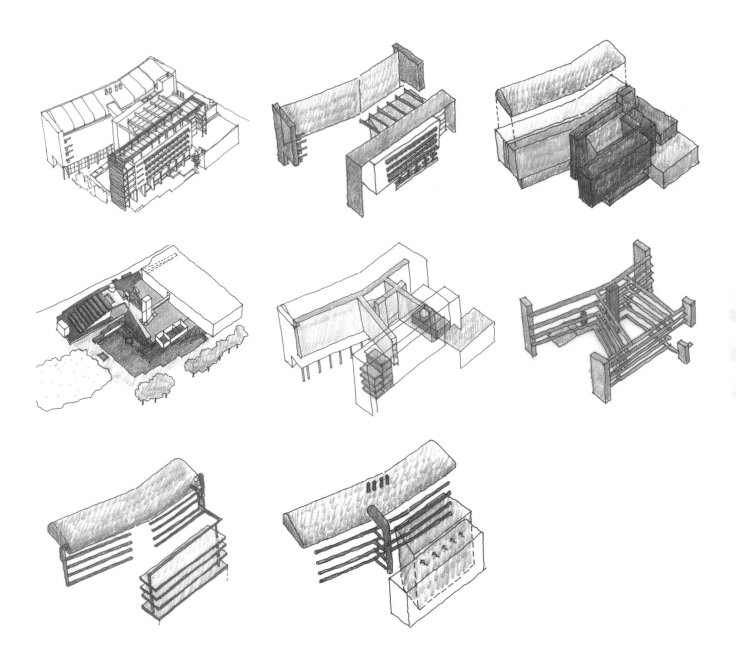

Facilities include general research laboratories, *an array of support and core labs, offices for administrative functions and computational research.*

The Fayez S. Sarofim Research Building is the newest facility serving The University of Texas Health Science Center at Houston. It is a comprehensive research facility on an urban site within the Texas Medical Center campus. The new building is designated to support research collaboration in the area of molecular medicine, particularly in genetics, proteomics and bioinformatics. The facility provides space for an initial population of 240 researchers, but ultimately will accommodate 450 scientists. Facilities include general research laboratories, an array of support and core labs, offices for administrative functions and computational research, a vivarium and appropriate support spaces.

Beyond its primary research function, the building provides gathering and assembly areas in the form of a soaring atrium and a 200-seat auditorium. All of the functions are connected by spaces specifically designed to encourage collaborative interactions. Planning, programming and design were all carried out with future institutional development in mind. The final design enables long-term flexibility and adaptability of the building to meet future scientific and research needs.

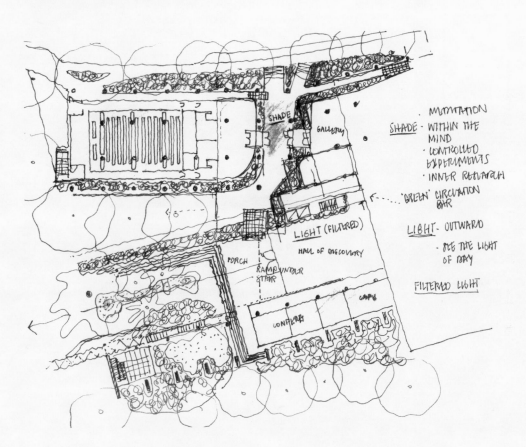

· MEDITATION

SHADE · WITHIN THE
          MIND
        · CONTROLLED
          EXPERIMENTS
        · INNER RESEARCH

···· 'GREEN' CIRCULATION
         BAR

LIGHT · OUTWARD

       · SEE THE LIGHT
         OF DAY

FILTERED LIGHT

SHADE

GALLERY

LIGHT (FILTERED)
HALL OF DISCOVERY

PORCH
RAMP UNDER
STAIR

CONIFERA

COMPLE

The principal client design team leader, Irma Gigli, M.D., and her colleague, *IMM Director Ferid Murad, M.D., Ph.D., established an open design dialogue with the design team.*

NO ONE KNOWS AS MUCH AS EVERYONE

The Fayez S. Sarofim Research Building embodies this adage and is the product of a unique collaboration between client and design team. The principal client team leader, Irma Gigli, M.D., and her colleague, IMM Director Ferid Murad, M.D., Ph.D., established an open design dialogue with the design team. The process was fact-based and exploratory. In seeking a solution that would elevate the mission of the Institute, the engagement of the scientists was crucial to the design, and, like the science within, the special qualities of the building reflect the intellectual connection between client and designer.

" It was possible to do what I've done simply because others did see what I saw. You can have a team of unconventional thinkers, as well as conventional thinkers. If you don't have the support of others you cannot achieve anything altogether on your own. It's like a cry in the wilderness. In each instance there were others who could see the same thing, and there were others who could not. It's an obvious difference we see in those who you might say have a bird's eye view, and those who have a worm's eye view. I've come to realize that we all have a different mind set, we all see things differently, and that's what the human condition is really all about."

Jonas Salk

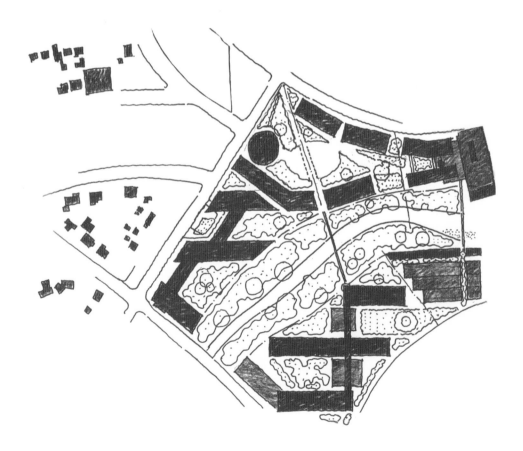

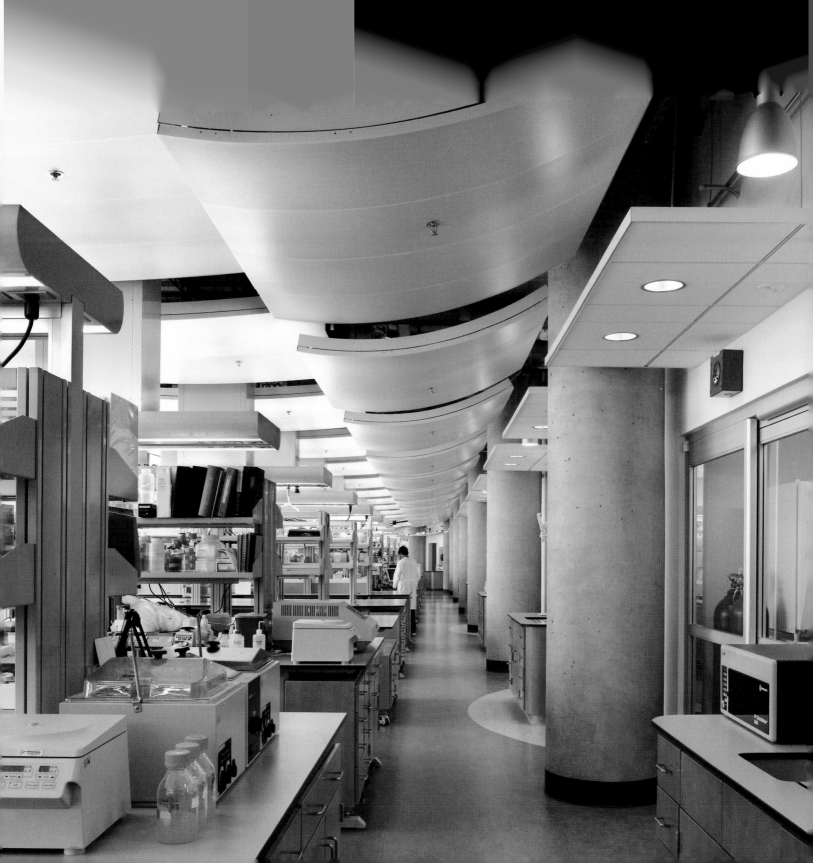

In this way, the building represents the evolution of
a model for encouraging peer interaction and cultivating community.

The IMM was founded upon the principle of collaboration among top scientists. Dr. Hans J. Müller-Eberhard experienced the benefits and energy of intellectual interaction while practicing in Germany and instituted similar practices in Houston. In the earliest examples of collaborative and interactive scientific buildings, the focus is on the laboratory space. With the Fayez S. Sarofim Research Building, collaboration and scientific interaction extend into the building's community spaces and connective areas. In this way, the building represents the evolution of a model for encouraging peer interaction and cultivating community.

The program and design of this building is symbiotic, as is the academic research: the building was designed with two wings—large, open laboratories in one wing are connected to a wing of offices via a network of open walkways. Similarly, the ground floor is open and expansive while the upper floors remain private and controlled. The building's wings and various levels are organized around a central, daylit atrium and other auxiliary spaces such as a central stair, auditorium, lobby, cafe, balconies, gardens and meeting rooms. All of these spaces provide opportunities for exchange and interaction, catalyzing a collaborative academic community.

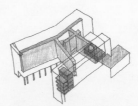

Upper-Level
Interactive Spaces

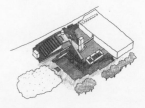

Ground-Level
Interactive Spaces

003 PROGRAM
NARRATIVE

The primary program function of *the Fayez S. Sarofim Research Building is flexible laboratory space for scientific research.*

The primary program function of the Fayez S. Sarofim Research Building is flexible laboratory space for scientific research. General multi-purpose laboratories comprise the largest area of research space. In addition, there are numerous core laboratories, specific purpose support laboratories, a BSL3 laboratory and a vivarium for use by research teams. General, core and support laboratories are located in the north wing of the building.

Office space for the research teams was designed to be flexible and accommodate workplace and computational research activities. Offices are located in the south wing of the building. Laboratory and office space are each provided with specific environmental control systems best suited for their specific programmatic needs. The scientific purpose of the building demands specialized systems to maintain critical conditions, a comfortable environment and uncompromised safety for all occupants.

The Institute Gateway is the name given to the spaces serving as the community hub. Its program includes the 200-seat Beth Robertson Auditorium, the Ben Love Foyer, the Hall of Discovery, the Judy and Rodney Margolis Faculty Lounge, a café and conference spaces. Building circulation serves an important function with the central stair, lobby spaces and walkways, designed to encourage informal interaction and socializing by occupants and visitors. In contrast to the highly controlled interior laboratory spaces, many landscaped outdoor spaces and terraces allow for relaxation, conversation and contemplation. In combination, all of these shared spaces reinforce the Institute's desire for the greatest exchange of ideas.

Laboratories	101,822 sf
Offices	22,367 sf
Institute Gateway	18,282 sf
Circulation	23,996 sf
Building Support	62,783 sf
Gross Building Area	229,250 sf

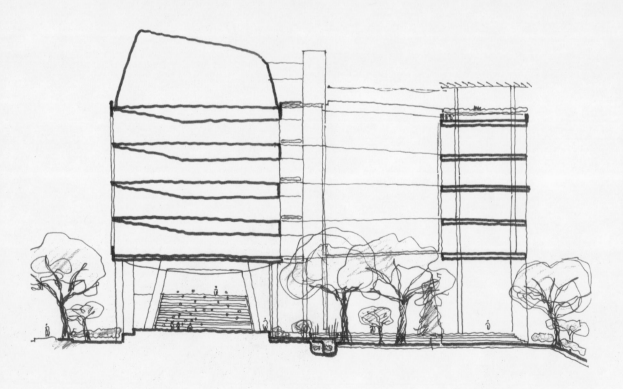

The process was the key element that
led the design from the initial idea to the building that stands today.

The entire team was committed to the highest aspirations for the new building. The process was a collaborative effort to seek a design response equaling the expectations and goals for the facility that were held by all of the stakeholders. The design team included representatives from each of the disciplines with complementary expertise. The equally large client group included representatives from The Brown Foundation Institute of Molecular Medicine, The University of Texas Health Science Center at Houston and the University of Texas System Office of Facility Planning and Construction.

The process was the key element that led the design from the initial idea to the building that stands today. To fully comprehend what was possible and, ultimately, what was the right course of action required a high level of participation from the client and users. The process was open and inclusive, founded in a method of holistic thinking called "integrated design," which is achieved both through organized collaboration between disciplines and through the interweaving and interconnectivity of building systems. Mechanical systems, the architecture of the spaces and the site conditions were all designed in synthesis. The result is integrated elements and systems, rather than one being appended to the other. At every level, preconceptions about research buildings were rigorously questioned by all stakeholders to ensure an appropriate solution. This comprehensive process required an engaged and willing client deeply committed to exploring new possibilities for both the design and use of the facility.

005 PLACE
HOUSTON + THE SITE

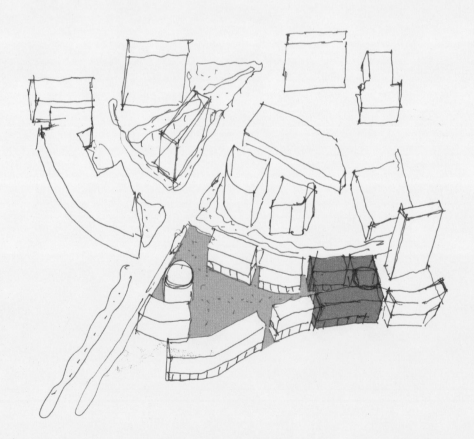

The site is prominently situated next to Bray's Bayou and adjacent to *The UT Health Science Center at Houston University Center Tower.*

Houston is located in a difficult climate that challenges every building with respect to issues of human comfort, air quality, periodic flooding and energy conservation. These conditions place enormous demands on buildings and supporting systems. The climate also challenges the typical sustainable design strategies for buildings of this type: fresh air ventilation is difficult to accomplish because of heat, humidity and poor air quality; the sun can be extreme and difficult to harness for effective interior daylighting; the area is prone to hurricane conditions that place stress on building and site systems. These circumstances both challenged the design team and made it clear why sustainable design strategies were important, not only for this building, but for the environment of the city and beyond.

SITE
The site is prominently situated next to Bray's Bayou and adjacent to The UT Health Science Center at Houston University Center Tower within the Texas Medical Center. It is surrounded by numerous research and patient treatment facilities affiliated with universities and healthcare institutions, and is close to established residential neighborhoods. The site is highly visible, provides opportunities for attractive vistas, is well served by roadways and is located directly across the street from the new light-rail line and a multimodal transit facility.

The site is susceptible to flooding, thereby necessitating careful planning and design to protect the new building from storm events and high water. The design of the site and ground floor purposefully maintains an open passage at the ground plane for air circulation and, in worst-case conditions, water flow. All research space is located above the ground floor, thus protecting it from flood conditions.

The site design creates an urban condition along the street façade and primary building entry. The entry is connected by the breezeway passage leading to gardens and a pool situated between the laboratory and office wings. The atrium, called the Hall of Discovery, opens to the gardens, protected outdoor dining and outdoor meeting spaces.

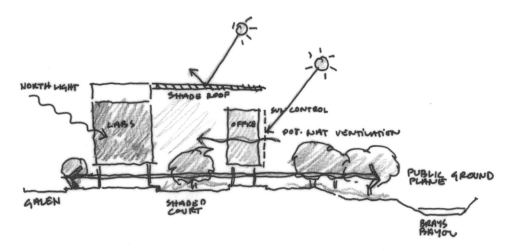

By separating office and lab elements, the environmental control system is able to *capture and reuse energy that would normally be wasted.*

The Fayez S. Sarofim Research Building was conceived as a 100-year building and incorporates sustainable design strategies at many scales. The building orientation allows optimum solar penetration and control of natural light. Fenestration and shading concepts vary appropriately with each façade orientation. The building was designed in section to optimize the spatial characteristics of different program elements. By separating the office wing from the lab wing, floor-to-floor heights could be set for each area, reducing the building volume and materials necessary for the office wing. Separating office and lab elements allows specific environmental control systems for each, while combining their source equipment provides the ability to capture and reuse energy that would normally be wasted. The atrium is tempered rather than conditioned by the surrounding conditioned spaces and by the office return air passing back to the air handlers. It is also carefully protected against solar gain by fritted low-e glass.

The building is designed to be a low energy-consuming building, and is expected to use 20-25% less energy than the ASHRAE baseline for similar buildings. The mechanical system is designed to provide comfort and high-quality indoor air for all occupied spaces as efficiently as possible. Each space type (laboratory, office, atrium, auditorium, etc.) is served

distinctly according to its needs and operating requirements. Because of the humidity and heat common in Houston, the systems are designed to harvest dry, conditioned air within the building. A single set of air handlers supplies air for both the laboratories and offices, reducing initial equipment costs and providing for efficient operation.

While prudent laboratory design demands a once-through air system, the office air is cascaded through the building to take full advantage of its high quality. The air serving the office wing is used three times. The first use provides comfort and conditioning to the office occupants. Part of that air is recirculated within the offices. Secondly, return air passes through the atrium, tempering that space. Finally, this dry, semi-cool air is recirculated through the main air handlers to reduce the outside air load. The laboratory supply air takes advantage of available clean office-area return air, and the office supply air has a high percentage of fresh outside air, resulting in very high air quality in all spaces while still reducing the overall outside air load.

Low-velocity ducts and low-pressure drop cooling and heating coils allow reduced fan horsepower and efficient operations for a building of this typology. Phase change sensible and summer latent heat recovery from lab exhaust air preconditions fresh air intake, reducing the amount of energy utilized to provide comfort and high air quality. Wraparound heat recovery provides energy-neutral reheat for the auditorium air supply. Evaporative spray coolers use captured condensate water. Proximity sensors at fume hoods control VAV exhaust. Daylight and motion sensors control lighting.

The reinforced concrete column and slab structure employs a high fly-ash content mix, thus reducing the upstream environmental impact of the building. Cladding and finishes are based on a palette of natural, sustainable and low VOC-emitting materials. The terracotta rainscreen cladding system provides a building envelope that reduces energy loss and gain and reduces the likelihood of moisture penetration. Provision was also made for future photovoltaic panels.

A district utility system serving the medical center campus provides chilled water, in order to take advantage of the economy of that large-scale system. Collectively, these features improve building performance, reduce energy and air loads, and reduce water consumption.

007 PARTI
BUILDING + CAMPUS

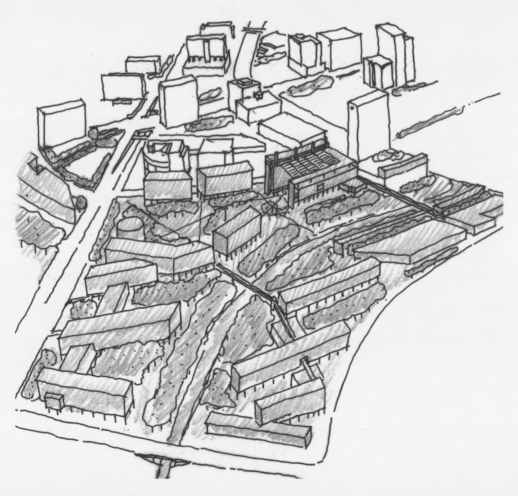

The idea for this plan is that of Jefferson's "academical village," which furthers the notion of learning as *a shared process that emphasizes the interaction between those involved in learning–researchers, teachers and students–as a key component in the pursuit of knowledge.*

The building anchors the east end of a future campus center. The idea for this plan is that of Jefferson's "academical village," which furthers the notion of learning as a shared process that emphasizes the interaction between those involved in learning—researchers, teachers and students—as a key component in the pursuit of knowledge. In the case of the IMM, a community of researchers, faculty, care providers and students are engaged together in biomedical research focused on disease prevention and treatment.

The gardens, walks and water feature establish the beginning of that campus plan. As the gateway to both the building and the future academic village, the ground plane is very architecturally open. The café, auditorium, conference facilities, service areas and lobbies serve the entire community, while the floors above provide closure and secure limits to access for the research and office areas. The building façades give form to the gardens and lawns, and the open ground floor and the secure massing of the upper floors work together to give shape and scale to the streetscape and future campus. This facility is at once both an entire community unto itself, complete with a sense of place, and an anchor for inviting future development within the planned campus.

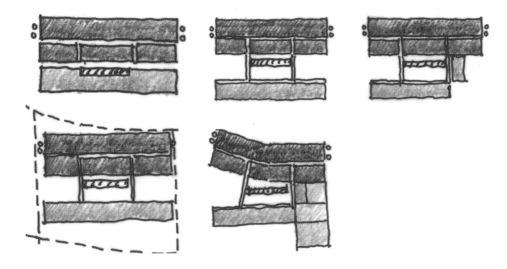

The building was conceived as a complex structure with discrete parts or species. *The five species are the Institute Gateway, laboratories, offices, the commons and the service building.*

The building design focuses on creating a dynamic, interactive environment conducive to research and learning. From the relationship with the outdoors, to the design of the architecture of the building, to the interior spaces, the approach considers form and function holistically, promoting the well-being and productivity of the building users.

The building was conceived as a complex structure with discrete parts or species. Each species was designed to house its individual functions and activities by having an appropriate space configuration, air-conditioning system, lighting design, furnishings and other qualities to ensure the highest levels of health, comfort, productivity and innovation. The passageways between distinct areas are designed to encourage and enable interaction and collaboration. The five species are the Institute Gateway, laboratories, offices, the commons and the service building.

INSTITUTE GATEWAY
On the ground floor, the Institute Gateway serves as the front door of the IMM and provides the building's public spaces—the central atrium or Hall of Discovery, the auditorium and lobby, the conference center, administrative offices, the gardens and outdoor breezeway. These areas are designed to facilitate informal dialogue among the scientists.

Visually connected, but above these spaces on the third floor, the Margolis Faculty Lounge overlooks the atrium. The club-like atmosphere of the room provides a comfortable gathering place for the scientists and has direct access to the roof garden.

LABORATORIES

The laboratories are housed on four identical floors, levels three through six. Designed to promote collaboration among researchers, each floor is organized in three zones that extend the entire length of the building: the north zone is a single, open research laboratory that is flexible and adaptable to any science related to the IMM's research mission; the south zone holds specialized research laboratories, such as hot rooms, cold rooms and other discretely designed shared spaces; and the central zone comprises alcoves that support the open, primary laboratory space. Core labs such as a high throughput lab, BSL3 lab, vivarium, NMR spectroscopy, fluorescence-activated cell sorters and glass wash are spread throughout the building to provide essential functions and services.

OFFICES

The offices are located on the same four floors as the laboratories but in the opposite wing. They are designed to provide a comfortable work environment that is a retreat for all investigators and research staff from the laboratories. The office floors are designed as flexible, open spaces providing views and daylight with access to an outdoor terrace.

COMMONS

The commons include the circulation and connective spaces that are integral to the design concept. Central stairs, lobbies on each floor, elevators, restrooms, outdoor terraces and connecting walkways between laboratory and office areas facilitate movement throughout the building and encourage informal interaction.

SERVICE BUILDING

The service building is located on levels one through three between the main elements of the building and the existing University Center Tower. This includes a loading dock, storage facilities, utility and service areas and future research support spaces on the first floor. Level two includes additional research space, and mechanical space occupies the third level.

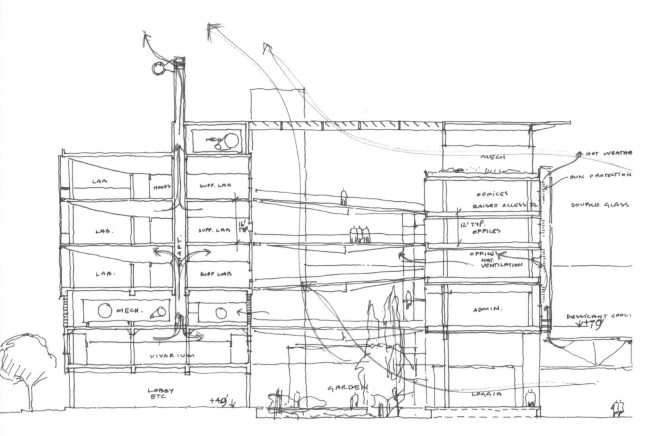

MECH.

LAB   HOODS   SUPP. LAB

LAB.   SUPP. LAB   16' TYP.

LAB.   SUPP LAB

MECH.

VIVARIUM

LOBBY
ETC   +49'

GARDEN

MECH

OFFICES
RAISED ACCESS FL.

12' TYP.
OFFICES

OFFICES
NAT.
VENTILATION

ADMIN.

LOGGIA

HOT WEATHE

SUN PROTECTION

DOUBLE GLASS

DESSICANT COOLI
+79'

The eventual design solution was selected because it best *embodied the mission of the IMM and supported integrated and sustainable design goals.*

Designers explored and considered many different strategies during the design process. The eventual design solution was selected because it was thought to best embody the mission of the IMM and supported integrated and sustainable design goals. The five building species and the site were composed in order to create a community of researchers. The concept, borrowed from Thomas Jefferson's idea of an "academical village," holds that the interactive process of learning that unites researchers, educators and students in a supportive and collaborative environment is an important component to the pursuit of information.

MODULAR PLANNING

The laboratories and offices are organized around modular planning principles. The lab module—in this case, established to be 11' x 36'—is sized for three to four researchers; large or small research teams are assigned an appropriate number of modules without the space management problems associated with fixed rooms. Constructed with standardized units and dimensions, the modular layout provides for flexibility and a variety of uses that respond to current needs and allow the nature of scientific research to change over time. The module establishes a grid on which partitions and casework are located. As modifications are required, due to changes in laboratory use, instrumentation or departmental organization, laboratories can be expanded or contracted without requiring reconstruction of structural or mechanical building elements. The planning modules may be combined to produce large, open laboratories or subdivided to produce small-instrument or special-use laboratories. The planning module also permits the organized and systematic delivery of laboratory piped services, HVAC, fume-hood exhaust ducts, power and signal cables to be delivered to each laboratory unit in a consistent manner.

Office space uses the same 11' planning module. Enclosed offices of various sizes are arrayed against the edge of the atrium and interior garden to the north of the office wing. Open office space lies along the southern edge of the office wing, which maximizes daylight and views toward Bray's Bayou.

BUILDING STRUCTURE

The building structure is cast-in-place reinforced concrete that contains a high percentage of fly ash to replace Portland cement. The structure is exposed and serves as a strong architectural element in interior and exterior conditions.

BUILDING ENVELOPE SYSTEM

The building envelope system was developed as a rainscreen. The underlying concept of this system is that it creates a pressure-balanced wall that eliminates an air pressure differential across the exterior wall and reduces the potential for moisture being drawn into the wall.

The building materials and systems include terracotta, zinc wall and roof panels, copper cladding, glass systems, reflective-membrane roofing and concrete roof pavers. In general, exterior materials are brought into the interior to emphasize the spatial continuity of inside and outside spaces.

TERRACOTTA WALL PANELS AND BAGUETTES

The primary exterior cladding is a wall system of red terracotta panels and baguettes that are attached to the building using a concealed subframe system. The panels provide a very durable outer skin that protects the resilient moisture and vapor barrier. The terracotta baguettes shade outdoor spaces, including the perimeter egress stairs.

ZINC WALL AND ROOF PANELS

Zinc wall panels protect the rainscreen system on the central service element and enclose the roof of the laboratory wing. The prefabricated system has a medium-gray patina that is stabilized and will not change color due to exposure. Zinc is also used extensively on the south elevation of the office wing as part of the shading elements.

COPPER WALL PANELS

The service building is clad in copper wall panels with a pre-patinated finish providing a green hue to complement the red terracotta and gray zinc.

GLASS WINDOW SYSTEMS

The building utilizes appropriate window systems for specific window configurations. The office and laboratory windows are aluminum frames with varying high-performance glass types that respond to the orientation.

The auditorium and lobby use cable-supported glass walls that span two stories, maximizing spatial transparency at the base of the building. The glass in the auditorium has specific acoustic qualities to provide sound isolation from outside noise.

The glazing in the atrium consists of a glass roof and wall systems. The systems are similar, as both are butt-glazed floating-panel systems with minimal visible support. The glass has specific performance characteristics and a ceramic frit in a dot pattern to significantly reduce solar load. Lateral forces are resisted by integrating bracing for the glass assembly with elements such as upper-level walkways.

ROOF MEMBRANE

The single-ply adhered roof membrane is a resilient self-heating product. Where it is exposed to the elements, it is white in color to reflect solar load.

ROOF PAVERS

Concrete pavers in multiple colors are used to protect the roof membrane where the roof is used as outdoor garden space. The pavers are installed on a floating-frame system to allow drainage below the walking surface.

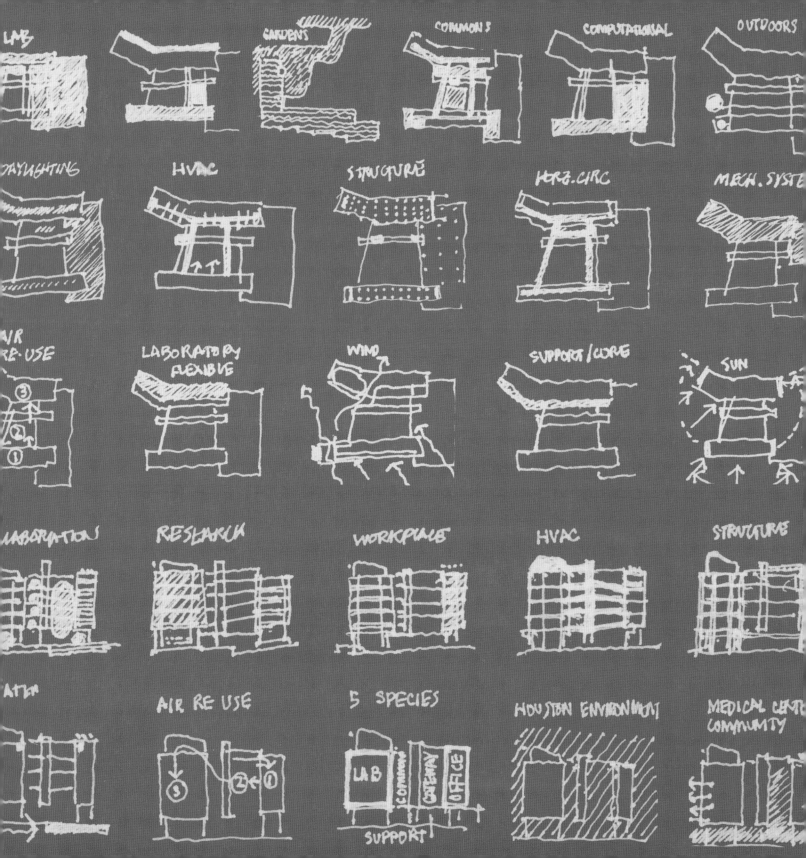

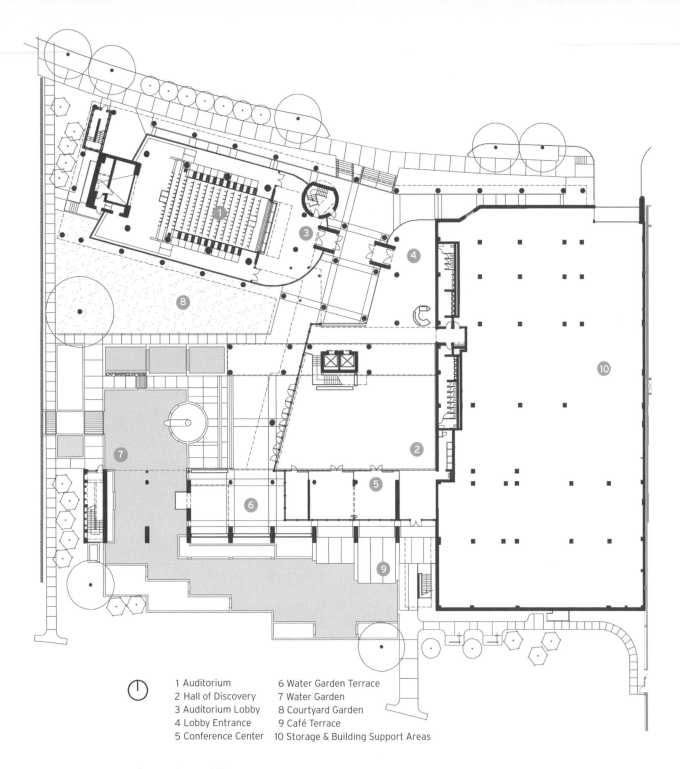

1 Auditorium
2 Hall of Discovery
3 Auditorium Lobby
4 Lobby Entrance
5 Conference Center

6 Water Garden Terrace
7 Water Garden
8 Courtyard Garden
9 Café Terrace
10 Storage & Building Support Areas

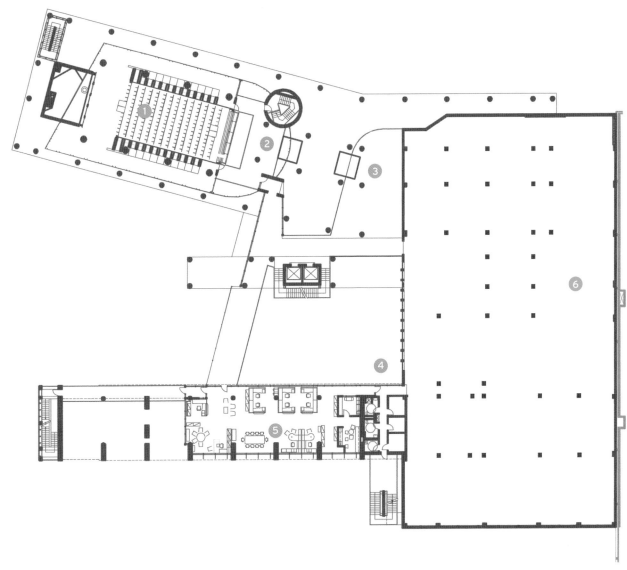

1 Auditorium
2 Upper-Level Auditorium Lobby
3 Lobby Below
4 Hall of Discovery Below
5 Administrative Offices
6 Research Support Areas

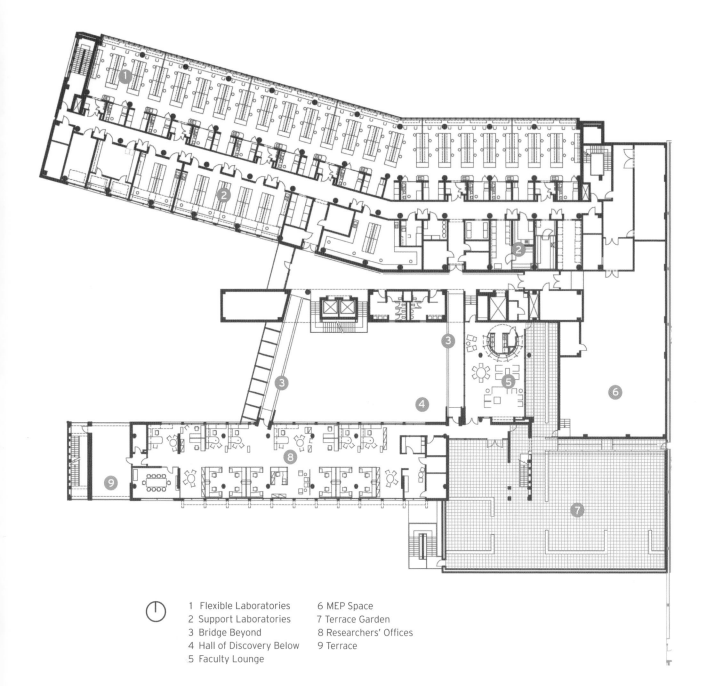

1 Flexible Laboratories   6 MEP Space
2 Support Laboratories   7 Terrace Garden
3 Bridge Beyond   8 Researchers' Offices
4 Hall of Discovery Below 9 Terrace
5 Faculty Lounge

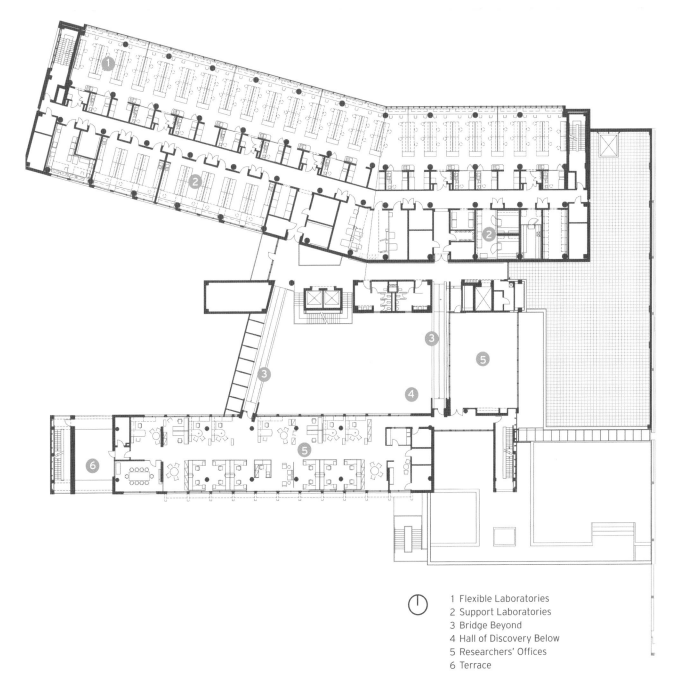

1 Flexible Laboratories
2 Support Laboratories
3 Bridge Beyond
4 Hall of Discovery Below
5 Researchers' Offices
6 Terrace

Typical Floor   99
(floors 4-6)

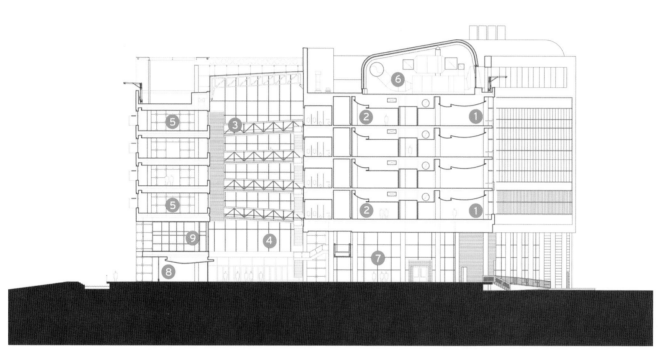

1 Flexible Laboratories   6 MEP Space
2 Support Laboratories   7 Lobby Entrance
3 Bridge Beyond   8 Conference Center
4 Hall of Discovery Below   9 Administrative Offices
5 Researchers' Offices

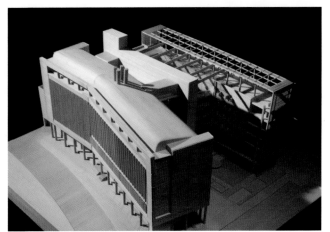

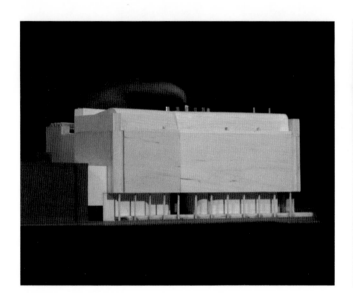

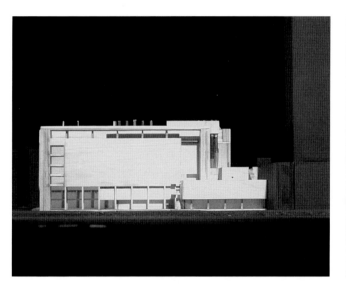
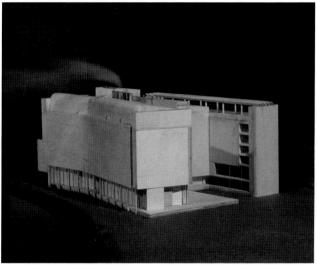

1   2   3   4

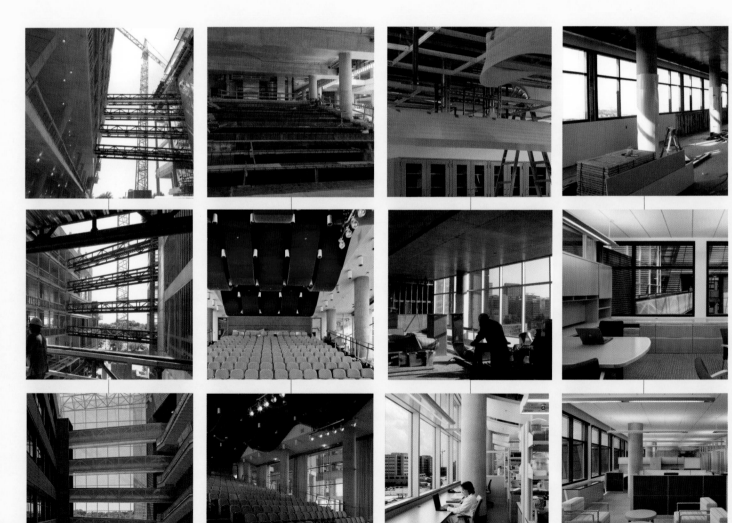

ABOUT BNIM ARCHITECTS :

BNIM Architects is a multidisciplinary architecture and design firm founded in 1970 in Kansas City, Missouri. Throughout its history, the firm has remained committed to its local and regional communities while establishing a national presence as an innovator of design methodologies, sustainability and new technologies in architecture, planning and workplace design. The firm has offices in Kansas City, MO, Houston, TX and Des Moines, IA.

BNIM's mission is to improve the quality of life for the owner, user and surrounding community through a balance of social, economic and environmental concerns. Without exception, the foundation of BNIM's continued growth and success has been the individuals—client and designer—who share a common vision and who find purpose in helping to create works of extraordinary quality and utility.

Through a process of integrated design, which is both an organized collaboration between disciplines and an interweaving and interconnectivity of building systems, BNIM creates designs that are both environmentally responsible and that achieve the highest level of design excellence. This philosophy, Deep Design/Deep Green, is embraced by all members of the firm.

As pioneers in the sustainable movement, BNIM and its associates have become known as thought leaders in the industry and beyond. BNIM's passion for sustainability has emerged on the national scene over the past two decades through early involvement in the U.S. Green Building Council and other national committees and demonstration projects. Their work helped define the national American Institute of Architects' Committee on the Environment, the USGBC's Leadership in Energy and Environmental Design (LEED®) Green Building Rating System and the Living Building concept.

BNIM's work has evolved to embody the concept of restorative design, which aims to maximize human potential, productivity and health while minimizing the consumption of resources and the production of waste and pollution. They design buildings and spaces that have a benign or healing impact on the site while being environmentally responsible, experientially rewarding and deeply educational for those who interact with them. Their projects demonstrate a belief that buildings and communities are and should be seamlessly integrated with the natural world. This results in structures that respond to and interact with their environment as living systems, celebrating light, water, landscape and natural materials.

Through research and investigation, the use of cutting-edge technology and the execution of solution-driven design, BNIM Architects has gained a reputation for design excellence. BNIM's projects, which include building and workplace design, urban planning and community redevelopment, have won numerous design awards from the AIA and other respected organizations. Included among them are national AIA/COTE Top Ten Green Projects Awards and recognition from the General Services Administration, the American Planning Association and the International Interior Design Association, to name a few.

bnim.com

CLIENT TEAM :
The University of Texas System Board of Regents. The University of Texas Health Science Center at Houston. Perry Graham; Jeff Carbonne; Richard McDermott; Dr. Irma Gigli; Gloria Horner; Barbara Hermann; Dr. Ferid Murad; Jack W. Smith; Nelson L. Horridge; Kurt Bartelmehs. **The University of Texas System Office of Facilities Planning & Construction:** Sidney Sanders; David Dixon; James Hicks; Stanley Scott; R. Eric Goelzer; C. Kyle Roth; Doyle Watson; Jamie Sampana; Jason McDaniel; D'Andrea Wade; LaWanda Jefferson; Damisi DeLaney; Charles Kieffer; James Da; Deborah Carruth.

DESIGN TEAM :
BNIM Architects (Architect, Interior Designer): Steve McDowell; Casey Cassias; Mark Shapiro; Mark Kohles; David Immenschuh; Bob Berkebile; Jara Kloucek; Filippo Castore; Christi Anders; Chris Koon; Kimberly Hickson; Brian McKinney; Mike Pollmann; Theresa Allinder; Julie Miller; Jim Miller; Sarah Hirsch; Joe Keal; Jennifer Isom; Gretchen Holy; Robin Dukelow; Barbara Cugno; Mohit Mehta; Rick Schladweiler; Phaedra Svec; Brian Rock; Gary Jarvis; Christina Assman; Curtis Simmons; Shawn Gehle. **Burt Hill** (Laboratory Designer, MEP Engineer): Thomas Donoghue; P. Richard Rittelmann; Jayesh Hariyani; Dave Linamen; Scott Lizotte; Jay Bullie; David Marti; Jason Decheck; Tim Bertolino; Alexandra Sokolsky; Craig Ashbaugh; Chuck Pichford. **Facility Programming & Consulting** (Programming): Terry Phillips; Doug Lowe. **Jaster Quintanilla & Associates** (Structural Engineer): Scott Francis; Gary Jaster; Brian Kirtland; Julie Hays; Tim Zhang. **Dickensheets Design Associates** (AV, Vibration Consultant): Ken Dickensheets; Amy Thomas. **E&C Engineers** (Local MEP Support): Jack Esmond; Heather Camden; Bobby Williams. **Clark Condon Associates** (Landscape Architect): Sheila Condon; Jamie Hendrixson. **Walter P. Moore, Inc.** (Civil Engineer): Charlie Penland; Manoj Adwaney. **Persohn/Hahn Associates** (Elevator Consultant): Ray Hahn. **DataCom Design Group** (AV/IT Consultant): Jodi Bole; Tommy Gairloff. **Rolf Jensen & Associates** (Code Consultant): Michael A. Crowley; Andrew Oldweiler; Debra Sue Miller. **Worrell Design Group** (Food Service Consultant): Rodney Worrell; Larry Wolfe. **R.A. Heintges: Architects/ Consultants** (Glazing Consultant): Robert A. Heintges; Piergiorgio Pesarin; H. Rok Lee; Till Houtermans. **WJE** (Exterior Skin Review): Mark Hopmann; Jerry Abendroth; Dale Clark; Brue Kaskel; Larry Meyers; Al Bustamante. **Busby and Associates** (Cost Consultant): Kenneth Busby; Bill McCauley; Rick Gerber. **Apex Cost Consultants** (Cost Consultant): Claude Eudaric. **Waterscape Consultants** (Water Feature Consultant): Harry Beckwith III; John Crowell.

AUTHORS :
Steve McDowell and Mark Shapiro
Introduction : Andrew Payne and Rodolphe el-Khoury

BOOK DESIGN :
BNIM Architects
Graphic Designer : Sarah Beshears
Project Coordinator : Erin Gehle

PHOTOGRAPHY :
Farshid Assassi, Assassi Production: front & back cover, pages 6, 7, 10, 24, 31, 32, 34-35, 36, 38, 40-43, 45,
46, 48-49, 56, 58, 62-69, 76, 80, 82-85, 87, 88, 90-92, 106, 107 -- Richard Payne: pages 8, 18, 26, 52, 60,
70-71, 73, 78 -- Pro Aire: page 51, 54-55, 106, 107 -- Paul Hester, Hester + Hardaway: pages 102-107

FIRST PUBLISHED by :
ORO *editions*
Publishers of Architecture, Art and Design

Gordon Goff & Oscar Riera Ojeda - Publishers
West Coast : PO Box 150338, San Rafael, CA 94915
East Coast : 143 South Second Street, Ste. 208, Philadelphia, PA 19106
oroeditions.com | info@oroeditions.com

Copyright 2008 ORO *editions*

ISBN 13: 978-0-9793801-0-5

DISTRIBUTION :

In North America	In Europe	In Asia
Distributed Art Publishers, Inc.	Art Books International	Page One Publishing Private Ltd.
155 Sixth Avenue, Second Floor	The Blackfriars Foundry	20 Kaki Bukit View
New York, NY 10013	Unit 200	Kaki Bukit Techpark II, 415967
USA	156 Blackfriars Road	Singapore
	SEI 8EN	
	United Kingdom	

ORO *editions* and BNIM Architects saved the following resources by using New Leaf Reincarnation
Matte, manufactured with Green-e® certified renewable energy and made with 100% recycled fiber,
50% post-consumer waste, and processed chlorine free: 37 fully grown trees, 7,974 gallons of water,
17 million BTUs of energy, 1,744 pounds of solid waste, and 2,948 pounds of greenhouse gases.

newleafpaper.com